Rodear y atravesar

Around and Through

Luana Mitten y Meg Greve

ROURKE PUBLISHING

Vero Beach, Florida 32964

www.rourkepublishing.com

PHOTO CREDITS: © Nicole S. Young: 3; © fred hall: 4, 5; © Cameron Whitman: 8, 9; © Marilyn Nieves: 10, 11; © creatingmore: 13; © kihoto: 14, 15; © Scott Williams: 16, 17; © Ina Peters: 18, 19; © David Stevenson: 20; © iofoto: 21; © Tyson Paul: 22, 23

Editor: Luana Mitten

Cover design by Nicola Stratford, bdpublishing.com

Interior Design by Tara Raymo

Bilingual editorial services by Cambridge BrickHouse, Inc.   www.cambridgebh.com

Library of Congress Cataloging-in-Publication Data

Mitten, Luana K.
 Around and through / Luana Mitten and Meg Greve.
    p. cm. -- (Concepts)
 Includes bibliographical references and index.
 ISBN 978-1-60694-385-4 (alk. paper) (hardcover)
 ISBN 978-1-60694-517-9 (softcover)
 ISBN 978-1-60694-575-9 (bilingual)
 1. Space perception--Juvenile literature. I. Greve, Meg. II. Title.
 BF469.K578 2010
 423'.12--dc22
                        2009016026

Printed in the USA

CG/CG

www.rourkepublishing.com - rourke@rourkepublishing.com
Post Office Box 643328 Vero Beach, Florida 32964

¿Rodear o atravesar? ¿Rodear o atravesar?
¡Vamos al parque, contigo quiero jugar!

Around or through? Around or through?
I want to play at the park with you!

4

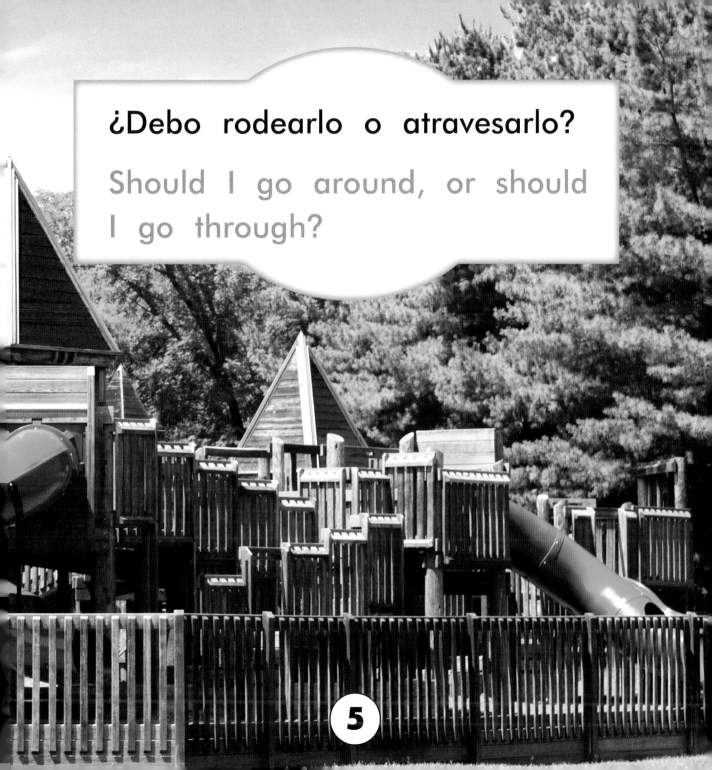

¿Debo rodearlo o atravesarlo?

Should I go around, or should I go through?

5

Veo una puerta. La atravesaré.

I see a gate. I will go through.

¿Debo rodearlo o atravesarlo?

Should I go around, or should I go through?

9

¡Rodeo el poste, no lo atravieso!

I run around the pole, not through!

¿Debo rodearlo o atravesarlo?

Should I go around, or should I go through?

Veo un túnel.
¡Lo atravesaré!

I see a tunnel.
I will go through!

¿Debo rodearlo
o atravesarlo?

Should I go around, or
should I go through?

16

¡Rodearé los columpios, no los atravesaré!

I will go around the swings, not through!

18

¿Debo rodearlas o atravesarlas?

Should I go around, or should I go through?

Veo las barras paralelas. ¡Las rodearé Y las atravesaré!

I see monkey bars. I will go around AND through!

21

1, 2, 3, ya ves...

1, 2, 3, look and see...

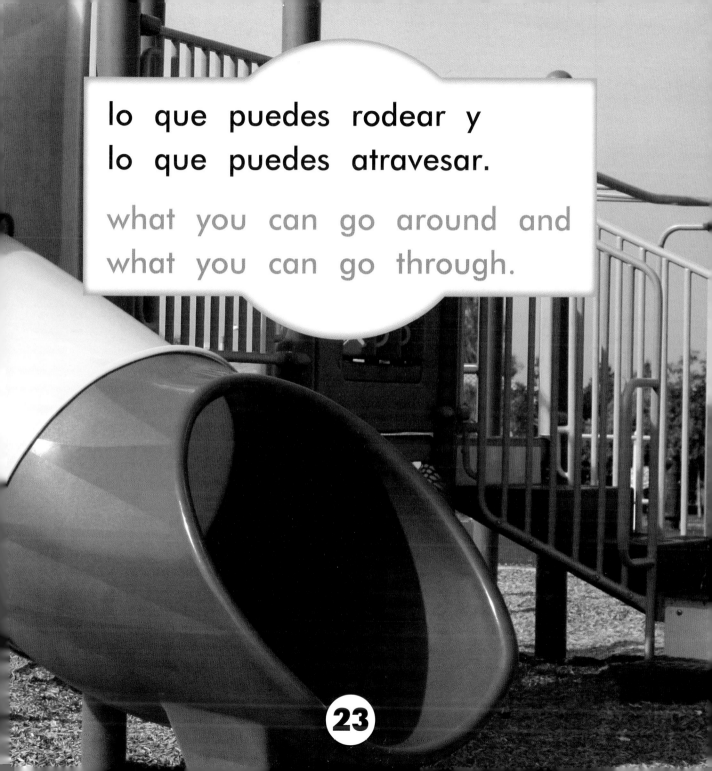

lo que puedes rodear y
lo que puedes atravesar.

what you can go around and
what you can go through.

23

Índice / Index

Visita estas páginas en Internet / Websites to Visit

urbanext.illinois.edu/hopping/rhymes.html

www.funbrain.com/brain/SweepsBrain/sweepsbrain.html

pbskids.org/arthur/games/poetry/poems/350440.html

Sobre las autoras / About the Authors

Por medio de llamadas telefónicas y correos electrónicos, Meg Greve y Luana Mitten pueden trabajar juntas aunque vivan a 1200 millas (1900 kilómetros) de distancia. Meg vive en la gran ciudad de Chicago, Illinois y puede jugar en la nieve con sus hijos. Luana vive en un campo de golf en Tampa, Florida y le salen pecas en la cara cuando juega en la playa con su hijo.

Thanks to phone calls and e-mails, Meg Greve and Luana Mitten can work together even though they live about 1,200 miles (1,900 kilometers) apart. Meg lives in the big city of Chicago, Illinois and gets to play in the snow with her kids. Luana lives on a golf course in Tampa, Florida and gets freckles on her face from playing at the beach with her son.

Artista: Madison Greve

24